GOATS!

A MY INCREDIBLE WORLD PICTURE BOOK

MY INCREDIBLE WORLD

Copyright © 2018, My Incredible World

All rights reserved. This book or any portion thereof may not be reproduced or used in any manner whatsoever without the express written permission of the copyright holder.

www.myincredibleworld.com

Photos Credits
Page 1. By Medena Rosa, available at https://unsplash.com/photos/teQlGfCSa0Q
Page 2. By Fachy Marín, available at https://unsplash.com/photos/_K-vAkMd9wE
Page 3. By Brian Holdsworth, available at https://unsplash.com/photos/pnIzzMjeYQg
Page 4. By Juliet Fix, available at https://unsplash.com/photos/8YnvueZYsRQ
Page 5. By Simon Matzinger, available at https://unsplash.com/photos/Gpck1WkgxIk
Page 6. By Jonathan Mast, available at https://unsplash.com/photos/3xLSyhkrJvE
Page 7. By Stefan Richter, available at https://unsplash.com/photos/FVgFuP3VgWA
Page 8. By Mikita Karasiou, available at https://unsplash.com/photos/XV5IEgh4bpM
Page 9. By Alvaro Reyes, available at https://unsplash.com/photos/l5FzEf1SDe4
Page 10. By Caleb Woods, available at https://unsplash.com/photos/EddYw_S1x14
Page 11. By Fineas Anton, available at https://unsplash.com/photos/C94_VgYo9vA
Page 12. By Hannah Markley, available at https://unsplash.com/photos/P507g0P9hag
Page 13. By Jonathan Mast, available at https://unsplash.com/photos/e3U2dYt526Y
Page 14. By Ricardo Gomez Angel, available at https://unsplash.com/photos/1n6TQYXq2UE
Page 15. By Dave Ruck, available at https://unsplash.com/photos/c1oDyH4m-9E
Page 16. By Quentin Kemmel, available at https://unsplash.com/photos/1ho06KfUpJ8
Page 17. By Harry Burk, available at https://unsplash.com/photos/ngzehCvVYdY
Page 18. By Soren Astrup Jorgensen, available at https://unsplash.com/photos/clSGD-GoHMM
Page 19. By Nicolas Tissot, available at https://unsplash.com/photos/pxdNENaNXO8
Page 20. By Paul Trienekens, available at https://unsplash.com/photos/kOhXZTbze2w
Page 21. By Manu Berbegal, available at https://unsplash.com/photos/uY4L-8gJs3k
Page 22. By Andrew Welch, available at https://unsplash.com/photos/3UI-q-GorIc

There are about 450 million goats in the world and over 200 breeds!

There are two types of goats: **domestic** and **mountain**.

Domestic goats live on farms or as pets all over the world.

Mountain goats live on the steep, rocky slopes of the American Northwest.

Goats were one of the first animals to be domesticated by people.

Goats usually live to be 15 to 18 years old.

Goats typically weigh between 125 and 180 pounds.

Goats are social animals and live in groups called **herds**.

Goats are **herbivores**, which means they only eat plants.

A male goat is called a **buck** or a **billy**.

A female goat is called a **nanny** or a **doe**.

A baby goat is called a **kid**.

Mother goats usually have 1 to 3 kids per litter.

Kids can stand up and walk within minutes of being born!

Goats' fur can be a wide variety of colors and patterns.

Goats don't have any top front teeth!

Goats are excellent climbers!

Goats' eye pupils are rectangular, giving them a fuller range of vision!

Goats have a great sense of hearing & can move their ears toward sounds!

Goats have a keen sense of smell, which helps them find food.

Some goats have horns and some goats don't.

Goats are incredible!

Made in the USA
Coppell, TX
20 January 2023